Some of These Days

Some of These Days

Poems

ROBERT KING

CONUN
DRUM
PRESS

AN IMPRINT OF BOWER HOUSE

DENVER

Poems from this collection, in present or previous versions, have appeared in the following publications:

Some of these poems first appeared in *Ascent, Birmingham Poetry Review, Cape Rock, Clackamas Literary Review, Full Moon, Future Cycle, Hiram Poetry Review, Louisiana Review, Louisville Review, Many Mountains Moving, Midwest Quarterly, Northeast, Portland Review, Potomac Review, Sleet, South Dakota Review, Wazee Journal*, and the chapbook *Naming Names*.

Library of Congress Cataloging-in-Publication Data is available upon request.

ISBN: 978-1-938633-21-8

10 9 8 7 6 5 4 3 2

This book is dedicated to poet friends who aren't around these days: Bill Borden, Bill Kloefkorn, Jay Meek, Ed Skellings, and Ken Warfel.

Contents

First Days

Last Days

These Days

First Days

Why I Invented War

Only because I had soldiers.
Given a set of lead cows, I would have
invented agriculture, the morning
driving to the fields, the evening back,

one barking dog, one herd-boy singing,
after I'd invented song, and strolling
back to the unruffled house. I would have
invented houses, drawn a spiral of smoke

from each chimney in town. Would have invented
towns. Would have invented fire for each hearth,
invented hearths, invented water to
put out fires, and because I had water

I would have invented flowers. But I had
only soldiers. This went on for years.

World War II in Omaha

1.

Incredibly enough, I listened to a boy
on the radio named Jack Armstrong.
Incredibly, each breakfast I ate Pep.

A plastic ring decoded messages
from an older man called Captain Midnight,
sentences I thought important from the dark.

2.

Playing canasta with the grownups,
I counted out amazement in the bright
living room with two full decks involving

a magnificent number of numbers,
fifteen hundred points just to begin.
Occasionally, we'd draw the curtains

and sit in the dark while outside sirens
cried at what might attack from the very air.
An only child, I played along with them.

Later, the happy lights came on: someone
would shuffle, whup, deal out a new game
and the world would start adding hugely up again.

3.

On the kitchen wall a Santa Fe Railroad
calendar showed a Navajo boy
motionless on horseback watching the train

frozen in the desert, plane hanging in sky,
bus posed on the highway. The train was gold,
the bus and airplane silver. The boy,

I thought, was thinking. Months fell away
below him. I didn't know what airplanes dropped,
what trains carried off. America advertised

how it could move and neither of us—
the jeweled watch of our precious futures stopped—
was anything but paralyzed at the sight.

The Day I Was Born, Nothing

The day I was born, nothing
in particular happened.
Picasso in that winter

of nineteen thirty seven
may have remembered swimming
last summer off the sand beach

of France, though not that someone
took the snapshot in a book
I find sixty years later.

Luise Ranier did not know
she would, the next year, win
an Oscar for *The Good Earth*

(nor did Garbo, Stanwyck, Dunne!)
Nor did young Dylan Thomas
on his honeymoon with Cat,

drinking and singing that way,
know what was ahead and those
were the great and famous ones.

A girl born three days later,
thin bones, brown hair, pretty eyes,
would attend the same college

I did and even, one night,
the same loud party although
with the complicated crowd

we would not meet forever.
Picasso, up to his knees
in the sea, looking around,

is in black and white and gray
like all of our photos then.
The next day grandfather wrote

in his diary it snowed. If
he had taken a picture,
the snow would have been white.

Picasso? Thomas? They were
years ahead, not thinking of me.
The same way I was.

Bobby

If I'd been a girl, my mother once mentioned
almost absently, I would have been Barbara,
laying in my hand a name I ate and swallowed,
like the twin edging beside you who died at birth.

That night, naked in bed, I tucked my little bag
of genitals between my legs, becoming
a kind of Barbara, a feeling I might
have forgotten by my seventies, but no.

I wouldn't have made a good wife as I didn't
make a good husband, but about the same
as a mother, talkative and concerned,
as I was a father, loving and careless.

Imagine Barbara lying in bed at night
wondering at her smoothness, pretending something.
Imagine someone who doesn't exist
thinking of someone who doesn't exist.

And, I will admit, there have been a few times
I felt a certain sadness for Barbara.
And maybe even for my one little self.
And maybe for the world. That's it. The world.

That Day

One summer morning, the child I used to be
felt eternity under his bare feet
warm in the backyard dust and sending warmth
up through his body to his heart.

I remember him practicing to be
a Baptist by pondering in bed
the kind of forever they talked about,
year after year after year,
until they vanished in his fuzzy sleep.

Forget what heaven was like.
Better the dust beneath the tree than heaven.
It wasn't even eternity, no matter what he thought,
but that one moment in that one morning
when everything possible stretched out
around him and night would never come
nor would another day and it was good.

At Fifteen

At the first hard shock, a first love
overturned in the instant of a letter,
I was burned by the hurt, if not

in the heart, that tight affectionate knot,
then in the chest, an ache swelling up.
That night I lay in bed watching the rain

burst over our small troubled trees
and cried, mostly from pain but partly,
that young, in tune with the storm's torrent,

until I stopped. But then, wanting back
that bitter pang, I counted up
every lost thing until I broke out again,

glorying in my new sadness,
delighted to feel it, to feel, my small life
as large as the worldly rain.

The Great Eighth Grade Uranium Hunt

Because it was the new gold
and lived in Colorado with us,
this was the plan: Albert, the future

engineer, would build a Geiger-counter,
piece by piece, which I, a future geologist,
would buy with my allowance. We envisioned

sandy wastes red with decay,
the ticks of the counter increasing
as we moved closer on foot

to our fortunes. This scheme lasted
two weeks, two pieces I don't remember.
We must have wanted to join our country's

dangers, in headlines or in landscape. Later,
there seemed something sinister in every
innocent aspiration we came up with.

I soon began investing in a jar
of maraschino cherries after school lunch
and drinking the tart scarlet chemical,

a dye I now discover has a number.
At the reunion, he was a minister,
smooth and gentle as a Bible's cover,

while I was a teacher of my own language.
I go to sleep sometimes thinking of the dark
long distances across America, the young

in their beds with their massive little secrets,
wanting to burn themselves with *something*:
whole life, half life, half of that, half of that.

Walking Home

Girls crossed arms to hold school books
against their delicate chests while
boys carelessly slung theirs, pretending
words weighed nothing, sauntering
down Myrtle Street, Mulberry,
coming together in groups
or couples, drifting apart,
and we felt those afternoons
that the beauty of living
might shatter us suddenly
into a blazing of light, if
we'd thought about how we felt.

Today, old, invisible
as the future, I watch them
gloriously amble, full
of themselves, bereft of math,
of history, still preparing
to break out into light, still
with no idea this is true,
moving away from each other
and nearing, a giddy pulse like
the opening and closing of hearts.

In Case Something Gets Stuck

"Here's some bread," my mother said,
"in case a fishbone gets stuck
in your throat," and here's some milk
if bread gets stuck in your throat
or wine, she wouldn't have said.

Here's some wind if an old song
gets stuck in your throat and here's
some love if you're stuck in yourself.

Here's a knife if your heart's stuck,
a heart if your soul gets lost
in the mountains, a mountain
if your feet are stuck in the mud,
mud if you've waited for rain,
rain if you're stuck in flowers,
a flower if trees are stuck
in the mall's concrete planters.

If a fishbone, if a stone,
a Bible, a single shoe
belonging to no one now,
if a dictionary, phone-
book of strangers, fountain filled
with blood, a little town, O
little town, my little town—

here's the way out if a map
gets stuck in your little throat.

Grandfather God

It's hard to be God, although you might not think it.
As a Boy Scout I helped plant hundreds of pines
on a graveled flat beside a river canyon road
and left them the way I was told, trusting in nothing,
apparently, because they never grew.
Hard to be God. Another time went better,
gathering Christmas trees to throw in a gulch
outside of town to stop erosion, catching the silt

the creek crept down. But then again we all do that,
slowing the weather around us, making the air,
even, pause for a moment with our bodies the way
trees do with snow, that smooth bowl around the trunk
that is one of the Inuit words for snow.
But that's not growing something up, not pines
or a garden, like my grandfather on summer
evenings, sitting in a curved metal lawn-chair,

sending an arc of mist over his south Denver lawn
and flowers and the pink papier-mâché flamingoes
he'd created which stared at the flowers even later
when he was dead. In fall, he'd gather the seeds
from Denver city parks, labeling them in small boxes
empty of matches used to light the hand-rolled cigarettes
which helped kill him too, and in spring the flowers
would grow again, thanking him and the Denver parks.

That day, following orders, we lifted seedlings
from a truck and buried them and drove away.
No one, even the adults, mentioned it after that.
Absentee, we tied knots in the church basement
all winter, our trees withering by the road the way
God's children might if not attended to on evenings thick
with flowers and cigarette smoke, the holy Denver water
arching its silver back to lay itself down on the ground.

College, 1849

Studying for an exam in history
long before I became it, I found
one page in my notes with nothing but
"1849" circled, re-circled, re-circled

by blue ballpoint, each swirl a pivotal
importance though I didn't know that secret.
Not even a college student would know
that's when Schlitz Brewing Company

founded itself and it wasn't the first
postage stamp in France delivering
a private letter or the U. S. patent
for the safety pin, those tiny inventions

nothing against the aftermath of Ireland's
Great Famine, black food rotting in the fields.
The Gold Rush, yes, was huge, thousands of miners
pulled to California (which President Polk

had won from Mexico) in one year, all that
much more important to us—that prospector
with a bewhiskered face, frowning or smiling
at the debris in his pan—than Garibaldi

proclaiming a red-shirted Republic
in February which lasted a few months
before a pope won Rome back and later
first declared himself infallible.

Poe, at forty, died on the bricks in Baltimore
after writing "Annabelle Lee", but not
immediately afterward, and Polk died too
after overwork and after cholera.

Speaking of death, the minié ball was invented
which, expanding on impact, made it better
and worse, an improved version becoming
the civil shell in our future Common War.

Still speaking of death: George Allen wrote "Bury
Me Not on the Lone Prairie", changing the words
of the previous poem "Bury Me Not
on the Open Sea." So after all the death

generally occurring, people didn't want
to be buried where no one could recognize
the place again, which, if you've seen the open
prairie or the lone sea, you can imagine.

Later, Garibaldi's wish for cremation
ended up in the dirt on his island farm
and Polk, buried in Nashville, later reburied
in his lawn, the old home settling into ruin,

will be dug up again, buried again
at the State Capitol which shows you can't
always get what you want even in death
although maybe Annabel Lee did.

I thought that year might have been connected
to the Industrial Revolution because
everything was somehow connected to that
but it may have been, I'm guessing now, that my country

first "stretched," as we say, (see Polk, see Mexico)
from a sea shining to a sea shining as it did
a hundred and sixteen years later when a kid
circled something really important although

he couldn't figure out why, his country
stretching and stretching around him, trying
to contain its multitudes of babies,
buried bodies, industry, gold, and blood.

Each year too many people died and too many
didn't in that public space around him. He
cared and didn't care, knew and didn't know, as
he studied, then studied again, his empty notes.

Guilt with Pears

Too early, perhaps, I read
Pinocchio who was wooden
and hungry with only three pears
his father sacrificed to him
who ate those up and begged for more.
Only the cores left he ate those—
I shuddered at him swallowing
the sticky fibers like fish-bones—
and then, unimaginably
enough, only the three stems left,
he ate *them* and was satisfied.

Thus, years later, whenever I eat
a pear there remains on my plate
the core's little wet hourglass
and the stem, a dark wink of thorn,
as evidence I've failed, not good
enough or hungry, failed because
of the luxury of my poor life,
never a real boy, never a man.

With Kenneth Koch with Helen in North Dakota

I remember when, to North Dakota, came Kenneth Koch!
He would read at the university, wittily, we expected,
after which Helen and I would take him to dinner.
But at the end of a three-day fight, driving to the reading,
we fell to shouting and I slammed the car to the curb
and Helen jumped out and I gunned it, lurching sideways,
scaring me about old cars and anger and even marriage.

I got to the reading of Kenneth Koch
and he read wittily and "urbanely" comes to mind
but I was sleepless from three nights, tired of myself
in North Dakota, so I kept nodding off as he read
much too far away and high on the stage—his poetry
should be read near by, although not confidentially—
and suddenly we applauded. Here was Helen!

The name of the motel of Kenneth Koch
was "The Westward Ho" with wagon wheels
propped up in the grass, a boardwalk to each room,
the restaurant furnished like a gold-camp whorehouse
with pewter plates and a profusion of red and gold curtains.
I was embarrassed I had slept, that I was married,
and that I was still loved, although mad at, by Helen.

I realized then that in New York Kenneth Koch
would have a lot of witty and urbane friends
who'd gather after a reading and their words would,
like a chandelier in North Dakota, light up a room
but when he asked how we thought it had gone,
we said several usual things, patting him as if
he hadn't slept in three days and was still mad at Helen.

Tonight, years later, I re-read "The Circus" by Kenneth Koch
and see him standing on a street corner in Paris,
which is approximately as lonely as one in North Dakota,
friends not yet gathered, Janice gone somewhere,
and, regarding a well-written libretto, he for a moment
loses his certainty of nerve "like the sun" and "the lack's
a black and icy night" and I am no longer with Helen.

Suddenly I am sorry for myself and Helen and Kenneth Koch
for when the streetlights blur and the traffic tosses in its sleep
and no one's there, it's damned bad, Paris or witty North Dakota
or another urban area, and I hope someone will be around for me
the way I wasn't for him and though most of all for me
I pray, whether it's Janice or Helen or someone else,
I pray that also happened for Kenneth Koch.

Coffee and the Existentialists

Life, this morning, is like trying to fold a newspaper in the breeze,
maybe waiting for a bus or at a sidewalk table,
where I am, maybe in Paris or North Dakota,
where I am, Jean Paul Sartre or someone climbing off
a box car across the street as a train slows through town.

The pages flutter as I try to contain the temporary news,
print aging so quickly it will yellow into an antique document
announcing World War II or even, in 1980, the death of Sartre.
The guy from the train, gray hair and a thick jacket, goes inside,
comes out with a glass of water, sits at the next table, contemplates.

In the 1950s a high school girlfriend's uncle
back from Paris told us how the existentialists danced,
worth a course in philosophy, good for a year of thought.
I continue doing my origami in the light tornado
of the cafe's corner and another arrives, a cyclist

with a helmet we'd have laughed at in the 1950s,
locks his bike, goes in, comes out with coffee, sits.
In khaki shorts, he has a tattoo of the earth,
inexplicably, on his leg. So three men have themselves
at three tables in the sun, and I'm still trying to read,

the news subsiding to tatters of gossip in my hands,
buckling, in a gust around the corner, like a large bird
whose wings I'm trying to subdue, remembering
riding my bike, not remembering riding a free freight,
and wondering what I thought my purpose was.

Years later, years, when I finally got to Paris
and sat in a new chair at Sartre's Deux Magots café
all I knew to say in French was "I want" and
"I'd like" so I sat there, wanting and liking everything
except later, standing at Sartre's and de Beauvoir's grave.

The cyclist says nothing, sips his coffee, and the hobo,
maybe, leaves to follow the earth, his plastic water glass
sparkling like fire in the air of the increasingly lonely corner.
The existentialists, if you want to know, danced straight
from the hips up, motionless, their feet and legs going crazy.

At least this is what Uncle Ed told us, his hands
fluttering, fingers impersonating their feet
like skittering birds, like newspaper pages
flying loose across the street, the tracks pointing
both ways, defining themselves by their existence.

That Life

The life I thought was mine
has walked off down the railroad track.

Oh, not like the hoboes I waved to
in the passing box-cars but like the boy

that walked the rails after the train passed,
heading toward my life beside the creek

that trickled under the shaggy trestle
and swam through grass before the highway.

I dreamed in the current's hush and flow
but couldn't remember what when I woke up.

If waking up is what, years later, I did.
Now in the suburb of a vanquished farm

I sit and wonder about that boy—
what could he possibly have been thinking

all those summer afternoons—and what
is he thinking now, having gotten up

and started back, that boy who never wondered
where the train, the creek, where even he, was headed.

First Light

Onto the street outside, light falls from
heaven, it must be, brightly. Window-wise,
     all I can see are the three floors
of the parking garage, shelves waiting
     for cars to line up like important cans,
and they, all ready, gleam. So what else

     is sacred in the street? A truck, "Distributing"
written on its side and angel-white, stalls
     by the curb. A blind girl walks with her dog
on her way not to be healed today and lo
     the morning newspapers arrive and nothing's
revealed on each, on every, given page.

     I guess only the falling light is holy. Although
I know light, strictly taken, does not fall, is
     simply arriving, both girl and pale truck glow,
the whole garage a ladder of glory
     the way some sunsets broken through clouds
into shafts made my mother think of saints.

     Otherwise myself, and remembering the warning
that if everything is holy, as it will be
     in a few more minutes, nothing is, I hold
my breath and step outside, ready for this
     final illumination, and walk away, my face
as shining as anyone's in the last of the first of the light.

Last Days

A Treatise on Light

By now everyone knows that a star may be extinct
the romantic night we see it, our hearts glub-glubbing
the way they do, but once at night in the mountains
I stepped from the cabin to relieve myself and muttered
"Forgive me" up to an eternal watch, both overwhelmed
and stewed with that sensitivity drunks have for the cosmos
or anything spinning around them. That sky was alive
and personal, on the grandest of scales, and looking down on me.

When I was thirteen, an evangelist promised the Last Judgment
consisted of a sky-wide movie of each poor life, the world at large
as audience which meant my girlfriend seeing what I did alone.
I would ache, I knew, for the film to jam and curl, to burn like hell.
Hearing the stars weren't permanent, I forgot about eternity,
having a new worry and, as I believed in everything
that made me tingle, I lay at night to watch one suddenly
wink out, but nothing was extinguished above our house.

The truth, I've been told recently, regarding light we see
is that stars die with a noticeable flourish of illumination,
not simply blink their pinpoints off. And this time is so vast
against the slow drag of space it would take longer than life
to watch one star brighten up and die in its dusty afterglow
which is not true, I've found, of anything else on earth
where, for example, people disappear at the speed of light.
Where darkness is they were, and where the brightness was.

Examination

It is science to see my father's skull—
as he lies in the dim machine next door—
on a screen, faint white, vague black, a pot
of thoughts, whether broken or not, the question,

and another science to see my father's skull,
an X-ray of the grave, the bare old bone
of everyone, jaw's jut, the forehead's curve,
the dark rounds that hold eyes, seeing or not.

He follows orders not to move. I barely
move myself. I shouldn't be seeing this.
I can't stop looking. This could be
a thousand-year-old find in a sandy cave,

the plates and fissures of our last design,
a round home held in the hands and turned,
the singular museum of memories
gone hollow, dry in the driest air.

"Wendell, wake up," the technician murmurs
into a microphone. He needs him awake.
The son, too, needs him awake, wanting
to see that unique familiar mask

pulled back over the general stone,
the temporary look a long time loved.
"Okay," he murmurs back, the soft wet eyes,
which I can't see on this machine, now opening.

A Sorting of Clothing

You must have seen a porch so filled
     with the hopeful despair of old dresses
the foundation has cracked, separating
     itself from the house like a doomed boat.

The heavy clothing of the dead wear out
     that way, slowly filling with a labored darkness.
On their suits, buttons are useless, anything
     which pretends to fasten itself around a body.

After father's stroke, my son and daughter help
     move him to the center of care and I sort out suits,
glancing as if passing them in a crowd, stuffing
     what to save in sacks, what to throw away in sacks.

Old shoes are awkwardly broken houses,
     their doors shattered helplessly agape.
If the shirts of the dead are new, it's too bad.
     If stained, a series of ordinary tragedies.

My children think the business is going too fast.
     Is the goal, my daughter jokes, to have no clothes?
And of course it is, to collect ourselves for years
     and at last piece by piece cast it away,

but I can't tell her that. Or that I'm ready
     for the same rough treatment, leaving old body
behind old body, cocoon, snakeskin, shell larger
     and larger, hangers of shirts on the slanting porch.

The styles of the clothing of the dead
     can make us cry, they are so happy
and convinced of their place in the world,
     each cut a decade we don't quite remember.

Coming home, I throw away a dozen shirts
        I have forgotten, pants not large enough,
dry shoes too cracked apart for service.
        What was I thinking, I think over and over.

When I visit father in the new room, we sit
        in our new clothes, not knowing exactly
what is missing, finally assuming nothing.
        At night, hundreds of miles apart, our shapes

collapse in the air behind us, designs in our bones
        decomposing. Lighter, the way we are with less
and with less, even surprisingly, we find nothing
        our clothing remembers to be fondly important.

At the Care Center

Outside what we used to call "The Home,"
the first fat snow slants across the windows,
a dozen residents grouped in their wheelchairs

to watch, some slumped sideways, the snow
passing dizzily from left to right, others crooked
almost upside down, the snow escaping

from the grass into the air, something leaving
the earth, relentless and forgetful, only
another of the day's incomprehensibilities.

*   *   *

Sitting beside my father
finishing breakfast, I'm aware
that the woman at the next table

feeding her husband
with an irritated devotion
has stopped to whisper to another

who eyes me up and down. "You look
like brothers," she announces happily.
The difference of thirty years seems nothing,

though sixty years ago it was a matter
of life and death and, sixty years later,
apparently the same matter.

*   *   *

A piercing soprano has come to sing
along with us. Because of the season
it's Silent Night. Because of the situation,

let her call us sweetheart. I mouth the words,
surely looking like I'm singing. Across the room
a man sings who may be mouthing the words.

Away in a Manger, You Are My Sunshine, songs
from childhood car trips, mother suggesting games:
titles with girls' names in them, with weather.

Now we are Sons of the Pioneers, tumbling
along with tumbleweeds. We warble that lonely
and free we'll be found, a certain truth.

*   *   *

The woman at the window is practicing
to be a tree on a windless day; another
rehearses the thought-struck look of granite.

Muscles sometimes tighten, making a look
of horrified surprise at something so long ago
only the dull shock has not been forgotten.

I study myself in my father's mirror
while he naps. I make a face, relax
to let it be my face again. It almost is.

*   *   *

The snow has finished falling, a thin
blazing bed made up for the day.
This has been a mild winter, not

what one would expect, the air
blue again, the world too bright to see
the way it is. We embrace, our faces

brush together. For now, I say goodbyes
and he says his. The same
with our love. Same words.

Birds and Death and Beauty

Buson once saw the iris-
colored droppings of a bird
fallen onto an iris colored
like the droppings of a bird.

I, on the other hand, see
a tired, red-haired woman, dyed,
I presume, deposit a handful
of letters in the mailbox

and enter the coffee shop
I'm visiting before seeing
my father. For an hour I think
of myself, then the world.

"I crook my arm, the world's crooked,"
wrote Takahashi—a sparrow
changing the universe—who's now dead,
born six years before father.

Later, we sit together
staring out of his window
either at trees the dark shade of earth
erupting into blossom

or the parking lot where cars
seem dead, a few birds dribbling
their pastels, sermon upon sermon:
how beauty comes when it comes,

how beauty goes when it goes,
how we can recognize it,
how we can sit and love in silence,
how silence is the last word.

Hunting, Mother and Father

One winter father, not yet father, asked mother,
not yet mother, along with him as he
went hunting rabbits across a deep-snowed field.
The story she mentioned twice, hardly a narrative,
was how he strode off with his long legs, she stretching
to fit each foot into the track his each step left.
No mention of the rifle or the hunt survived.
There were, as far as the details went, no rabbits,

simply the fact of two people trudging through snow,
unmatched but managing to match, and I was not
yet following behind, stretching out my legs
in exaggerated giant steps, like a game,
following the blanks in the snow where they've gone:
simply the open field and its small absences.

Night Watch

One of the few lights given us in the dark
I can identify, Venus shone directly above
the highway the night I drove toward my father
after the stroke, car wreck, not sure he'd live,

not certain of anything. Younger, I'd truly believed
in the Evening and Morning star which turned
into a single old planet wandering around.
Earlier yet, it was easily obvious to worship,

name it for harvest or lust or a god murdered
by morning and each night born out again,
but these days there is profound faith
its clouds of heavy atmosphere are acid

no deity would ever dare to breathe.
Tonight I'm camped on a river bank
in prairie back-country, the fire gone down,
Venus so low ripples of broken silver

lead over the slow mumbling water
enough to make me think walking across
would not be a dangerous miracle. My father
does not remember he didn't die

nor even, in particular, that I arrived,
and nothing's named in space like Aphrodite,
so this shine of twenty million miles
shouldn't seem companionable. I know the sky

holds welcome only because familiar, but,
only because familiar, it also holds farewell
and I am trying to learn from Mother star
and Father, sleeping alone on the edge

of the land, how to leave the earth the way
the murmuring dark river floats itself, carrying
that light, a code repeatedly breaking itself
into these splinters of unintended holiness.

Choosing Where to Leave

1. The Corso Death Scene

Gregory once told me that
if he were on the street and knew
he were dying, he'd slip into
a movie, didn't know why.

So there were assumptions:
a theater nearby, the right time.
Well, we know now his way
didn't happen—daughter's house,

hospital. I thought, reading the news,
that a movie would have had
the comfort of closed darkness
and he'd have been with others,

a whole roomful staring at lights,
at color, with music, everyone
talking and talking on the screen,
a movie about being alive.

2. Clouds

I've always hoped I'd lie
out on a hill the time death rose,
busy with the clouds and their rich
transient concoctions, the way
they boil up with luxurious names,
while dying, and that sharp blue.

3. The Stupid Tree

But it will be, outside, some stupid tree
and then I will not "see to see,"
as Dickinson described. It will be chance,
an insignificant tree with no intention
or lesson or maybe part of a terrible formal garden.

4. The Theater of Trees

Their leaves will shine like broken pieces
implacably. They will not care
about death, even their own.
And the lights will go out slowly
in the cramped rooms of the leaves,
like small theaters darkening
except that in real life, the lights
come on again. Gregory, wake up.
The colored musical clouds have moved on.
Everyone has stopped talking now.

The Graves Empty, The Graves Full

At the name "Sea of Galilee"
      I lift up my eyes to the television
illuminating the find of a Neanderthal burial,
      fourteen adults and a child,

shells strewn across her ribs, red ochre
      staining her tiny enduring bones,
who thus lay when Herod owned this air,
      Gabriel, near these broken cages,

settling on Mary with his proposition,
      someone creating wine, adding up bread
and fish, gliding across the thin surface
      of belief, promising he'd die, promising

he wouldn't. Trying to discover our grandmother,
      a cousin sent probes into the Wisconsin earth,
which stopped at nothing, her grave empty
      as miracle, its stones rolled away, so when

we visit the family at their small granite addresses,
      they may not be home, only a few
surviving death in bogs, a vault of ice,
      dry hidden caves dark as Scripture.

Millennia before Eden, they picked up and came
      here, stout and powerful, brains the size
of Peter's, Paul's, but heavy browed, muscular,
      nothing like the painting in my church,

Jesus, soft girlish hair, white gown, lifting
      a lantern in some dark woods,
knocking on the door, we understood,
      to our stony hearts. It is a matter

of accepting they never entered the kingdom,
        who were not our ancestors but lived with them
"in harmony," the television reports, who also
        started fire, cared for the sick and lame,

the first to bury their dead, scatter shells
        on a child's breast, to daub
her bones the color of old blood. Oh men
        of Galilee, why stand ye looking up?

a wind asked of disciples, and I look down,
        trying to imagine the grandmother
I don't know, the grandchildren I do,
        in remembrance of this very girl,

the familiar bread of her flesh, the wine
        pulsing through her veins. Dust in our hearts,
the world broken around us, constantly
        resurrected, we all live the same life.

These Days

Some of these Days I'll Miss You

And, honey, I'm halfway there, although today a man
 lifts a plastic chair from his truck by the artificial lake
along the artificial Interstate in Nebraska
 and sends out a line, communicating
with the placid dark smoke of the water
 and I remember an early morning of fog
on the coast of Portugal watching men wading
 hip deep along the rocks to pick up something
from the salty little crevices in another language.

He doesn't cast again. This is lake-fishing, a yellow
 and red bobber bobbing yellow and red,
both of us waiting, watching the water. Once I saw
 a gaggle of photographers troop down in Spain
to set themselves beside a bay of picturesque
 and one, there's always one, who set up his tripod
to photograph photographers photographing the bay.
 Watching the man I remember watching the man
in New York, looking down at his two windows

across the street as he set up a chessboard in one,
 then disappeared, appearing in the other,
getting glasses, a bottle of wine, disappearing,
 appearing in the other to set them out.
Later, having forgotten he was alive, I looked down:
 two men playing chess, amazingly drinking
the wine which had been rain at some time,
 perhaps in Spain where a woman watched
out her window, looking forward to something.

"The things you remember," my father shook his head one day,
 a man whose life had gently narrowed
to a room along a hall of rooms—smiling almost
 in mistrust. He had left remembering the day before
behind. The current news was someone opening

a puzzling door, the way light slanted through.
Finally his accomplice, I sat with him, searching
    out the window past the bird feeder always empty.
And today I sit by proxy in a white plastic chair

looking at my line in the lake and the lake's line
    mirrored back in its window, an unfinished completion.
The highway hums behind us with thousands
    of steady purposes and I am living on the verge of leaving,
a good thing, I have decided, to practice.
    Some of these days you'll miss me and, honey,
I will too although I've forgotten where you are
    but I'll find out. Highways, unlike lakes, are good at that.

These Days in America

The young man, farm-boy type and blonde,
comes to my outside table and asks,
because I'm smoking a cigar,
for a cigar, and lingers, talking:
just out of jail this morning
(for breaking probation) he has
the bland unknowing innocence
of the more quietly disturbed.
"Stole a cigar from a store once,"
he remarks, "that had these pilgrims on it.
What kind was that?" And I don't know.
"And a wagon," which doesn't help.

Then a girl arrives, both at the shelter
these days, she's ADD and on her meds,
he's off of his. She's a good worker,
she insists, but somehow can't keep
a job—that's why she became a dancer.
Although I'm not sure of that logic,
I can't keep from imagining her
peeled and skinny under colored lights
until the boy asks for another cigar.

Finally they rise and leave, the way
our grandparents, the pilgrims, wrecked
the Mayflower on Plymouth Rock,
stole a few wagons and jostled west,
smoking as they came to the Promised
Jails, who shed their clothes
and began their job of dancing
wildly, guilty and guiltless,
almost naked in America.

Two Conversations with the Schizophrenic

1. Memories of Nietzsche

You could say that the "schizophrenic,"
he told me once, although on his meds,
talks to himself at the outdoor coffee shop
but that's not it. He talks to someone else.
 "What do you think of that?" he grins
into the attentive air, then turns to me.

Somehow it involves Nietzsche who wrote,
I assume, the well-thumbed book he carries,
notes sticking from its grimy pages,
but I don't know Nietzsche well enough
to follow him. When I read it in college
I felt like I was listening to
a schizophrenic talking dense paragraphs
interspersed with sips of espresso.

I waited to see what the professor said
about this guy spilling out his ideas
at an almost superhuman pace
but he waited too and the other students
rolled their eyes, wishing, by God,
they were outside drinking coffee
but, let me tell you, that doesn't help.

2. The Old Norman Soldier Business Again

He discovers I'm reading poetry.
"I'm not sure of the over-riding context,"
he starts, then pauses, not having found
the right voice to repeat. "A good metaphor,"
he starts again, "can change your way of thinking,"
and I wonder at the changes in his thinking
before I wonder about my own.

"It's like a door that's dark," he offers, "but
you can see light coming through the other side.
Even though you may not have the key."
I jot this down so the next thing I hear is
"The Norman soldier's eyes are dead,"
and after a few stunned seconds I realize
he's describing the ash on his cigarette,
"A profile, mostly white ash, with long hair.
His mouth is on fire with words."

For a while, we listen to our own voices.
"There's understanding," he breaks in, or out,
"and then there's wisdom. Understanding
is in the gut," he says, and I, not believing
I'm doing this, ask where wisdom is.

Waves

And one wave was forbidding
and the next giggled as it breached.
The sand sucked down the foam
with maybe a mournful sigh
but the waves attracted attention
then dispelled it with collapse.

It was an inviting afternoon
we hadn't been invited to
and on the horizon—sometimes called
the "apparent horizon," that curve,
like a plow blade where sea and sky
don't meet—there slowly moved

a cruise-ship where people we didn't know
were dancing, although probably not,
of an afternoon, so they might have been
swimming in a tiny tub of water
above the ocean's huge one, an irony,
of course, but often unnoticed these days

and anyway if you're swimming
you're mainly aware of your exquisite skin
and the measured pressures of your breath,
how you let it out or haul it in,
how you can 'hold it' as if your hand
grabbed that air and clutched it tightly.

As children we vied to hold our breath,
a kind of elemental contest
with no rewards and nothing, we thought,
you could get better at, just a test
of whatever we were born with, but we
have forgotten what we were born with

and are no longer 'little children' so Jesus
might have a different opinion of us
now that we know 'suffer them' means 'permit,'
not the painful verb we at first imagined
although maybe not many of us wondered,
awash in the metaphorical swimming pool

of our own lives lurching only slightly
above the rolling depth beneath us all.
And I said "Let's get a drink" and stood up
and you said the bar wasn't open yet
which I realized was true and sat down.
And so we stayed where we were, one wave

showing the architecture of smooth ruin
we were oblivious to or splashing
a joke at our feet which we didn't get,
and the ship had ploughed on like childhood
and we went on breathing, swimming or dancing,
whatever it is that moves us in and out.

The Funny Traveler in Omaha

When I put up, by association of parts,
my umbrella I become Portuguese
along an Omaha street because I

bought it in Portugal, a Saturday market
in a small town, men standing in clusters
on one side of the street, the women, mostly

in black, on the other, a divided village
in separate knots, two sides for marriages
to get away from each other.

Suddenly in the market there came a downpour
and I was standing beside the seller
of big umbrellas and if it had rained

all day—and I had places to go, I couldn't
stand around not-talking to the men—I was ready
although it only rained three minutes so I had

this large black sculpture to carry around two weeks
but now I can use it in Omaha,
light drops ticking like a dozen watches

on the tight drum-skin of my contrivance.
Let's face it, the umbrella is comic,
the funniest amenity we've made.

The duck, of course, is the funniest animal,
not mallards but the children's barnyard-book-
duck, he and she of the orange bill and feet

and the white plump decoy of a body.
The bicycle is the funniest machine,
if you're keeping a list, because all its parts

are so visible. A car is mysterious,
or a jet, because its parts are hidden
but if you've looked at a bicycle you can

make one although perhaps not a good one.
An umbrella is comic because
it's that obvious a thing. There's also

a certain sense of self-importance one exudes
carrying an umbrella and someone else's
self-importance is also funny

the way I am now, under my umbrella
in the fragile rain which is not like the drench
on Gene Kelly in a street in "An American in Paris,"

the first movie I took a girl to, Jayne, a Baptist, who,
when I remarked on the way home how exciting it was,
though going with a girl was the most exciting part,

said she thought it was very "carnal." Who
but a Baptist girl would use that word? I'm sorry I left
Jayne or she left me but not really, so long afterward now,

but I am sorry I had to leave the Portuguese market
and I'm also afraid, no one else on the street
carrying an umbrella, that I'm surely

a comic figure, an old duck riding a new bicycle,
because although it shows I'm well-traveled
no one else knows that and I think of singing

a chorus or two about rain and Jayne
but (see under "Umbrella, comic") I'd look
even funnier and to all of Omaha.

Mendelssohn, with Birds

I find out Mendelssohn wrote his Great Octet
    at sixteen. I'm seventy-four and counting
the syllables of backyard finches
    but you don't want to hear about me.
You want to hear about the finches.

There are finches in the Octet, warblers,
    brisk sparrows, swans—how they look swimming,
not how they sound—and chickadees and doves,
    robins twirping, although there's some scrubbing
in the violins. I mean, the blackbirds.

A week ago I found a wind-blown nest,
    inside its broken shell a half-formed thing,
1/100th the size of a piccolo,
    beak opened grotesquely for beautiful
reasons, a small intelligence struck dumb.

The trombone refuses to sound unless
    it is blown, unlike a piano, attuned
so even the sunlight trembles its wires,
    or the loose snare drum which, even untouched,
can scratch a rattle in an empty room.

That bird, barely alive, was a tiny
    ravaged piano, its raw muscles tense
as wiry snares. With nothing left to save,
    I walked away from what must have been
both its surprise at life and then at dying.

Mendelssohn's parents gave parties, for one
    of which he wrote the Octet. At sixteen,
remember. At sixteen I was eating
    pigeon stuffed with sage from along the fence,
no parties, no piano in the parlor.

We played "Fingal's Cave" in high school band,
    "Mid-Summer Night's Dream" in orchestra, and I
am sorry I didn't read or know his name
    and that no teacher let us in on it.
What would we have felt if we'd been told

the piece for today was written by a teen?
    I like to think that we in our little nests
would have dug right in in honor of our gang
    and for all possible composers who,
bereft of an orchestra, twittered unheard.

We call a bird's noise "song" because we don't
    know what the bird means. We call something
an octet because it takes eight people,
    all wearing the same suits like the finches
in the backyard now, taking their seats,

industriously tuning themselves up
    before I rise on stage, tap for attention
and lift both arms, collecting the whole backyard
    in that breath-held moment of silence before
they begin, with their miniature throats, to sing.

Maybe the World's Widest Tree

We were going to see the widest tree
in Mexico, a strange distinction,
but first I wanted a beer. You must
plan these things. Then we went.

It was wide. I bought a postcard
with I don't remember how many
proud schoolchildren stretching
to hold hands around the trunk.

Surely, an old gentleman sits in a bar
right now, boasting mistakenly (in Spanish)
"When I was nine, I had my picture taken
in front of the largest tree in the world, damnit!"

I'm writing this while looking at a large tree
in Jackson Square in New Orleans and resting
from an arthritic knee. I've never lived
near the biggest anything or tallest

or even the smallest, everything its normal size.
I was the normal size, and both knees worked.
Now an up-standing street guy passes
with strings of beads picked up from the gutter.

It's the Wednesday after Mardi Gras, workmen
unhooking the bleachers, sweeping up
the colored fragments of celebration.
Although you could say a tree is like

the body, or vice versa, trunk and arms,
Rodin said the human body is a church,
maybe like this St. Louis Cathedral
fronting the "large open common used at times

for military parades and later
as a market place," where now hundreds
of artists may gather to sell their work
although today there are only three or four

card-tables where Tarot practitioners
wait patiently for tourists to read
and finally I stand up a piece at a time,
my body stone by stone building its own

particular denomination,
and walk away from the largest tree
in sight, bereft, perhaps, in my childhood
although look how much it helped the guy

to be photographed, kids holding the hands
of their tiny friends and smiling out at the earth
with all its average trees, no one around
to celebrate the future, or even read it.

Apples of the Poet

The poet said I could come out to his place in the country and gather
    windfall apples.

Another friend had found a cider press and invited others so I was in the
    market for apples, but whatever I expected, it was not these:

freckled and pocked, pied, worm-bitten, dappled, dazzled, shrunken,
    with patches of yellow and green and red.

Each apple could have been one of his poems, each particular in its
    diction, offering "delights," offering "shadows," which would one day
    win a Pulitzer.

So I left with two heavy paper anthologies of apples and later, in the city, I
    turned the wheel that crushed the lumps into a dusky yellow juice
    and sat with the others.

The poet had quit smoking and drinking years before. Just think of Keats
    with all his cigarettes and Scotch—no, that was me, not Keats.

Then think of Keats lying sick in his little rocking death boat waiting to
    leave for Italy day after day.

The juice was the color of troubled sunsets in Italy shining on old
    windows—the taste a "mellow fruitfulness" of harvest as we
    gathered all we could before the winter.

I drank—although some had gin and tonics that warm afternoon—until
I was almost sick of it, my shirt stained with a golden smoke, my
hands thick with stickiness.

And then I, never to win a Pulitzer because I had not been writing
poetry all my life—I had not done anything all my life—helped
clean the press and washed up and went home, lugging a couple
of volumes of murky juice

that tasted delicious, as will any essence crushed and drunk, and that
looked—like any natural beauty—as if it would rot in a week.

Cats and the Crusades

We stayed in the town in Portugal
where some crusades started
and there was this cat.

It had rained lightly all day,
and the restaurant that night
had a balcony outside, wet and cool,

so when a cat pushed open the French doors,
or the Portuguese, it let in also
a chilly draft felt by a man

at the nearest table, back to the door,
who, still talking, pushed his hand
behind him, and closed the door

almost. In a few minutes the cat
pawed it open and went out,
the man almost closing it again,

still talking. During the Crusades
cats, dogs, horses had their own functions
to attend to, while whoever ran things

headed south to regain some place
and someone died, a dog didn't worry,
a cat wasn't mildly surprised, a bird

had somewhere, as they say, to get to.
Again, our cat came back in, everything repeating.
We were nervous and agnostic.

We knew if we did not finish dessert soon,
ice-cream and port wine, body and the blood,
we'd be caught in how history happens,

forced to murder, repent, and murder,
rain after cold rain on stone,
cat after Christ after cat.

Objects of Manufacture

Among these objects of manufacture—meaning
we factured them together with our hands—the Street
of Asphalt, the Walk of Concrete, the plastic sign
for Wine and Spirits, Payday Loans, I could go on,
among all this there is visible of nature

the sky, naturally, and two small trees
in a little landscape of mown grass—Dine In
Take Out—which are real trees, so it's not the hotel lobby
with artificial leaves including, in the best hotels,
a few artificial dead leaves which seems something

only God would have thought of but although I remember
the Fall in the Garden of Eden I don't remember fall
in the Garden of Eden. "You shall labor in the dust,"
or whatever it was God said, big on dust those days,
who maybe added "Unless you invent asphalt or discover

the combination of concrete." Which we therefore
after several centuries of sandals did, and after more
enough of God was left in us to order two pines
from the Garden of Nursery and arrange for a crew
to dig a hole in the fill, the dust, and sock them in.

The Payday Loan company has locked its doors.
A pigeon alights on a billboard, "Carryout Special,"
and almost abruptly leaves. The bricks of the one-story shops
have been joined so long we cease to notice them.
But two trees lift their hands to, let's say, heaven,

the quietest prayers I've heard. Let us have Wine to lift
our Spirits but let no one ask for another payday loan.
There is no miracle today but this, these trees and that we may
dine in or, having our freedom, out and by "out"
we usually mean back home somewhere. Let's say it's home.

The June Issue of *Poetry*

I'm reading on the back porch when the squirrel
comes down the garage roof to the bird-feeder again,
my shooing so familiar by this time he won't move
unless I come up really close but today I have

the June issue of *Poetry* in my hand and I stand up.
I'm only eight poems in, so I hold the thick part
of unread poems and flap the eight at him (five
already about writing poetry) and the flapping,

being something new, something about a few "O!"s
scattering in his direction, an "amethyst," a "form-
less," scares him off the roof. And I sit down. Although
it's the June issue of *Poetry* it's only May

although it feels like April, as more than one person
has said this week, including me at the hardware store
where I did not buy a squirrel-proof bird-feeder
or even my June copy of *Poetry* but two bags

of cypress mulch for the flower bed which has now
been spread with the ragged rich stuff. I am reading
again—though trying to remember what color is amethyst
and why in the middle plains I have cypress mulch

from, I assume, Louisiana or somewhere Whitman went—
when, wouldn't you know, the squirrel is back again
with a couple of "O!"s still on his fur like stars
or the fallen blossoms of the spirea which are beginning

to snow down the way the white tongues of peony petals
loosen and fall which could be an example of the poem
surrendering itself, line by line, but which seems
to me more like a pale house collapsing slowly

from age, gray shingles and boards giving away to the air
inside a forest where no one hears or the prairie
so open there's no sound anyway or, more accurately,
a place in the grass where someone has murdered a dove,

I am not a poet today although, having looked
it up, I'm reminded that amethyst is purple and,
looking further, find it was considered a remedy
for intoxication, for people who ran around

shouting "O!" I guess. The June issue of *Poetry*
doesn't need another poem about itself, although
it might want a few about red cypress mulch
or the tenacity of squirrels or Walt Whitman

or the birds that haven't yet come, pale doves,
or May and how, in a backyard at least, all life
gathers and falls apart, gathers and falls.

Rain, the Names Of

In Greek there's the rain a parent feels
for a child, the rain between husband
and wife, between brothers, a certain
unseemly self-rain, and the rain showing
God's concern for us, and for rocks.

*   *   *

Virga, rain not reaching the ground,
a name for something that
almost doesn't happen, quickly
doesn't exist. Most of our names,
matters of fact, are like that.

*   *   *

At the highway cafe for breakfast,
everyone speaks of waking up last night
because of the rain. I, driving through,
cannot know that rain or their sleep,
or their love for each other at waking up.

*   *   *

Some rain falls hidden inside clouds,
gets airily lifted back before we see it,
forms again, falls, fails again.
By the time we see it, the rain is old,
the rain has lost its memory.

*   *   *

In the city, a man sells umbrellas.
In the Japanese painting, everyone
has one. In the Rockies, I crouched
under a pine, the rain speaking Japanese
softly in strings of light and dark

*   *   *

Once I read a book on the history of rain.
It seemed to be a long book
but it wasn't. Nevertheless
it took my whole life
and the lives of everyone else.

Mozart's Impresario Overture

and a severe weather warning
this morning on the Interstate:
storm gathered and a gathering
form. I can stop art with a flick
of the dial, my life with a turn

of the wheel at a mile a minute
but it's the cloudy swelling of snow
and air, that none of us, nor Mozart,
can certainly halt, a helplessness
we move through trying to forget.

Overtures are introductions
but think of how many exist
without whatever they began,
like these clouds, lowering ahead,
only a light slit to drive through.

The opera was basically
a singspiel, "surrounded by
spoken dialogue" (how I seem
to live), and lasted one half-hour.
The libretto was in German

but, constantly re-written, who cares?
If you want something permanent,
try any weather leading to something
else, always itself. The Impresario,
I cannot forget, has been re-arranged

for a quartet of clarinets
and I remember a blizzard
when I thought nothing else would come.
For now the wind arrives and more
of the wind, having its own spiel

to sing, more words and snow over me
faced with something that could end right now
or not, death by freezing or beauty,
my life and Mozart's and the life
of the morning's moving moment.

The Man From Another State

is at the door, holding a knife
he stabs cheerfully into the heart

of a ruby grapefruit, carving
a clean slice out, a sacrifice

as impressive as the taste.
As he talks I become an expert,

one of the few who can savor
whole histories of flesh, of juice.

Later, I can't prove to my wife
why we have two crates of grapefruit

in the basement, where he and I
have decided would be best,

but I know the porch seemed emptier
after he went back to the orchards

of Florida, blue-acid sky, its sunrise sea,
where men happily eat with knives

in their hands before they fan out
in trucks across the country, sly

and confident, where other men
wait behind doors for someone

to come with a line of patter,
promising to cure their poverty.

What I Do For Others

I need my wife around—I think
tonight, as I wash the pan I fried
bacon and potatoes in—to cook
for her, in which case I'd poach
a little sole with a Korean
dipping sauce and maybe some baby
greens just touched with vinegar.

This is the way I help others,
how I satisfy the dentist's
compulsive worries over my teeth,
the doctor's concerns for my health.

Almost every day I stop by
the Loaf and Jug where the clerk
needs money but is afraid to ask
so I give him some, although to shield
his embarrassment he hands me one
of the cigars he's hired to guard.

And sometimes, wife away, I eat
at the little café downtown
so the waitress has someone
to call honey. After I leave,
she feels warm and full all night.

Another Secret of Life

Driving to work, I hear on the radio that someone has discovered the oldest living "creature," as they say. I'm on a one-way street with timed stoplights, gently jockeying for position in the stream of things, in my jacket pocket a list of elemental food—milk, bread, eggs—to buy on my way back home. The early sun glares through my dirty windshield so I can barely see.

It is also difficult to see at the murky bottom of the Gulf of Mexico where lies a tube-worm two centuries old. It is described as the size of my finger and six-feet long, a creature who lives in a chitinous tube, like the shell of a shrimp, who has no mouth or guts, ingesting nutrients from bacteria living around it.

Scientists may want to study it, the radio says—as I smoothly glide through another green light, things are going well today— to determine the secret of longevity. Although I think the secret must mainly have something to do with lying without a mouth in a tube at the bottom of the ocean, I find the image of the worm entering my thoughts throughout the morning, absorbing its food in that passive darkness longer than I can live or my children. Or.

All day it grows heavier, older. By late afternoon when I have purchased milk of the mother, bread of the father, and eggs of the holy spirit, I feel it underneath me, a smooth strange root of the tree of life curling in darkness around the world, all the rest of us mere dreams of the worm at the center, or thoughts, or flowers of light, perhaps, completely out of its view or concern, so perfect a God He no longer cares what goes on above Him.

Shoes

Shoes are a symbol, I once thought, looking down
at my young lover's Birkenstocks, tiny boats
of love moored by the bed while she showered,
poignant, but when she put them on, I forgot them.

(I am not speaking here of the one high heel
found in a hotel elevator, or the lump of a shoe
rumbled over on the highway, or two
tied and tossed to dangle, helpless, from a wire.)

I have worn in my life clod-hoppers, gun-boats,
white bucks, blue suede, oxfords, boots, penny-loafers,
sneakers, tennis-shoes, sandals (like Christ
I first thought—later, like Allen Ginsberg).

Of course we think about shoes mainly when they're off,
in a muddle by the front door, the kids' tumbled
in a corner, or your love's empty lovelies, or yours
when they're tired, parked in front of your chair.

Later, our shoes slip-on or have Velcro tabs
so we don't have to fumble with those first lessons.
At the last, someone takes ours off. We won't
need them anymore. Death, you see, is soft.

A Perfect Ten

Because this is, I guess, the Age
of Information, I now know—
from my CD notes—the Ravel
adagio lasts ten minutes
and three seconds, and I wonder
why the Bournemouth Symphony
with Andrew Litton pianist
didn't make it an exact ten,
surely only a tiny push
needed here or there to bring
the whole orchestra in by deadline.

That trickling half-dissonant
background could be condensed, the pulse
finding a melody could have
found it more quickly, that chord,
face it, does not have to be that long.

But maybe the delay comes in
the last three seconds, so I wait
until it arrives: a flute
lifts, cutting a curve in the air
before it alights and changes
to a somber oboe, its last
resting place, a far piano
fluttering in high octaves.

If I knew I would live only
ten more minutes, alone tonight,
let's say, the phone useless, no help
anywhere, maybe I'd listen
again, although I wouldn't hear

those final three unnecessary
seconds. They would be the rest of life,
while my eyes glazed up like a flute,
silver and cold in its soft case,
my ears full of almost silence
like a darkened auditorium.

Coming Up with the Last Word

What is eternal, anyway? I am tired
of saying it's never a true adjective
to everyone and will begin to answer.

It is well-known autumn leaves
are not, except on the atomic level.
We will not be on that level here.

I pass, without comment, mountains
which melt, stars tending to explode.
Coffee is frequent, but it is not

eternal, whether hot or iced.
A paper clip is eternal if you lose it.
Anything lost is eternal.

The look on my dead friend's face
at twenty-three has been eternal
to me, although I am not.

They say the triangle's idea is eternal,
the drawn pencil line not, but the shavings
in every old classroom sharpener's

little bucket might be eternal, the idea
of a triangle on its last legs already.
It is time to quit kidding around.

What is truly eternal is the shining
of rocks in the mountain streams
I remember as a child. Not the rocks,

those worn colored things, nor the illusion
of the stream, but the sheer shine
shining always, always that light.

"No Ideas but in Things"

—W. C. Williams

And I immediately agreed
because, back then, I had
only a few ideas but a lot
of things multiplying themselves

and this has continued as I age,
assuming this yellowed leaf a thing,
the slow river it fell into
another thing, examples of

being and becoming,
words I've never written
in what might end up a poem
if the river comes in again.

The river—that was easy enough—
is not confused nor is that leaf
spiraling downstream confused
or even dizzy although I'd be.

In these parts, our TV forecaster
yearly reports the best days for "color,"
the idea of autumn a fluttering lure,
and people brightly troop to the hills,

deliciously glorying in
the glorious deaths of little things.
And here's another thing, another
leaf, that is, in the same water

which we know is never the same.
Oh, the pines pretend to be ever
and ever green although they slough off
their dead so subtly the fiction

continues even in my mind,
as close to having an idea
as I can come up with, the sturdy
mountain opposite another

eternity, granite's decay
so painfully slow we don't count it.
The best time to view the colors
of the mountains' gradual death

is every day but few of us
are interested: anything
long-lasting is forever enough.
And here they come, the next two leaves

angling around in the current
without resistance to the river
which offers no resistance
to the rocks nor do the rocks resist.

The river is not an idea
although, under this yearly waste
of gold, it contains ideas
and at the bottom rest, or not,

ten thousands of stones and I don't
understand, although these days I try to,
the implacable wisdom of all these things.

The Aspens of America

Or I could sit here, which I decide to do, outside
the motel in the same-shaped curving white plastic chair
I see everywhere in America, and look out
across the parking lot at the aspen in the breeze,
admiring their characteristic small fluttering
because of their flat stems joined at cross purposes
to each leaf which causes that quaking like little hands,
like the Queen's back and forth wave but not in slow motion,
and, as the yellow leaves are roughly triangular,

I think of the triangle metaphorically
where we give the three points names, one of which was Julie,
and remember the only psychiatrist I ever saw—
insurance would pay for nothing less—that long summer
who said he'd usually dealt with dyads but this
was triadic which almost sounded like "terrific"
or something with three wheels, like Julie and Royce and me,
or me, Julie, and the baby, or, weirdest of all,
the baby, the Royce, and the me. The psychiatrist

said I should take up running—he ran every morning
and felt, he said, "like I make the sun come up," which sounds
like grandiosity or some condition as well,
of course, as a generally wholesome good feeling,
trotting on the edge of the stage of night and slowly
bringing the footlights up and the spot, let's not forget
the spot, on him, or a spotlight on Royce, no, he had
no dialogue in that play, although an early draft
had him asking "Who was on the phone?" and Julie lied.

The term tri-angle is quite transparent—you can see
in the word what it is. *Rectangle* is different,
from the Latin *rectus*, right, and *angulus*, angle,
which sounds like something a choir would sing, the *Rectus
Angulus*, but this has nothing to do with angels,

whose root means "messenger" though the leaves might mean that too.
Now a husband and wife traverse the parking lot's tar
and I know, as they near their small temporary door,
that they are the most important people in the world

as far as they are concerned which is true and nothing
to feel badly about or scorn because they don't know
Royce or what his story was, or mine is, or Julie's,
too far removed from their Brad attending school, their Nan,
a teen at home, now babysitting for the Baxters.
The Baxters have three aspen in their yard and sometimes
Betty looks out at the troubled leaves but Bill doesn't,
or if he did, would never consider them troubled.
That's the trouble with you, Betty has, on more than one

occasion, remarked. But Bill does not consider it
a trouble or even a minor failing because
he knows if you start out interpreting everything
in the world, psychiatry or Latin, a baby,
the sunrise, the movement of leaves, for emotional
meaning you'll never get down to the bottom of it
which he refuses to do and forgets about it.
Forget about it. After I get up, the white chair
stays there, waiting for all of America to sit down.

The Rock in the River

It's just upstream, above a series of riffles
smoothing out into a pool, and I've watched it
being covered by the June rise, uncovered

by the July falling. Some weeks the water
floods over it, sunlight glinting flashes
of warning, and some weeks its awkward shape

is a lost body floundering up and down
but today a little spout of water shoots up
two feet high and I find this unusual

until I see a trio of boys, shirts off,
taking aim and I realize it has
turned into a battleship or some such

target for a missile and I remember
one time doing the same thing in this river
with two friends and how we tried to hit the rock

but were more than happy when it missed because
when you hit it nothing much happened, a little
"tick" and you saw your rock fly up or break,

but when you missed there was a satisfying "glug"
as it plumbed the shallow depth and then produced
an eruption of more than satisfying spray

which is more than happening now, the game changing
to an unabashed heave of heavier stones
so the huge explosion splatters closer to them

bringing shrill cries and the reason I've gone on
so long is that they've gone on so long—imagine
if I were watching a marriage or an empire—

and they show no sign of quitting so what I'll have
when my fingers finally tire like their arms
or their attention is some words about this moment,

these many moments, repetitive and changing
at the same time, like the sunlit river itself and
although I'm almost finished now the boys are not

so be assured inside the coming silence
that a rock hits water somewhere in the world—
and someone exults in that eternity.